30 Days of Resilience Journal

Kathleen Fanning

Copyright © 2023 Kathleen Fanning
All rights reserved.

No part of this publication may be reproduced, distributed, or transmitted in any form or by any means, including photocopying, recording, or other electronic or mechanical methods, without the prior written permission of the author, except in the case of brief quotations embodied in critical reviews and certain other non-commercial uses permitted by copyright law.

Independently published on Amazon

ISBN: 978759466895

Photo credits:

I want to say thank you to Niamh Mason for her many, beautiful images.

All other images were made using Canva Pro

Acknowledgments:

Thank you to Anne Devine for allowing me to share excerpts from her wonderful book 'Encourage Yourself, Encourage Others'. You can reach Anne at
info.devinepublishing@gmail.com

Thank you also to my wonderful VA, Janine Harris janine@virtuallyauthentic.com for helping to create this book from my thoughts and to Karen Brown karen@coachkaren-brown.com for bringing it all together twice!!

Dedication

To my wonderful 'board of directors': my husband, my sister, brother, sisters-in-laws, nieces and nephews and all my friends and family who bring me joy each day.

"All shall be well,
and all shall be well
and all manner of thing
shall be well."
~ Julian of Norwich

Contents

Introduction and welcome 1
Day 1 3
Day 2 7
Day 3 11
Day 4 15
Day 5 19
Day 6 23
Day 7 27
Day 8 31
Day 9 35
Day 10 39
Day 11 43
Day 12 47
Day 13 51
Day 14 55
Day 15 59
Day 16 63
Day 17 67
Day 18 71
Day 19 75
Day 20 79
Day 21 83

Day 22	87
Day 23	91
Day 24	95
Day 25	99
Day 26	103
Day 27	107
Day 28	111
Day 29	115
Day 30	119
Final words	123
About Kathleen Fanning	124

Building *Resilience*
when you need it most!

INTRODUCTION AND WELCOME

Hello!

This 30 Days of Resilience Journal was created in 2021 to support making the positive changes to build your level of resilience.

I wrote this in the context of emerging from the pandemic and all the challenges that brought with it. Two years on and we have been found to be amazingly resilient! But perhaps, for some people at a cost. In various ways – covid still is affecting many.

Yet…despite it all we have come through those difficult years and hopefully are looking ahead with some positivity and optimism. The world continues to be challenged - sadly with wars, poverty, and the natural disasters we are experiencing as a result of Climate Change. There is really so little we can control in our lives, yet we can control – or manage our thoughts – and that can make a huge difference in our lives. Managing our thoughts is one theme in this Journal along with other supports to build our resilience.

At various times we all can feel that our 'well of resilience' has been depleted and when that happens our Saboteurs or negative thinking can take hold. The Survival part of our brain is overly

Building *Resilience*
when you need it most!

cautious - always pointing out what could go wrong. That is what it is meant to do – its job is to keep us safe from real or imagined threats. Resilience draws on more than caution though, it is what helps us navigate 'turbulent waters' helping us to bounce back and hopefully emerge even stronger.

This Journal will guide you through various aspects of Resilience through the use of images, quotes and my personal reflections. Every day has a different theme and a tip or action for you to try out each day and then write about on the Daily Journal pages. It takes a minimum of 30 days to create a new habit and my hope is that following this Journal for 30 days will begin to embed these new practices (or reinforce existing ones) and that they will really become lasting habits!

Finally, if you'd like to discuss any of this with me or learn more about what I do – please drop me a line at kathleen@kathleenfanningcoaching.com and have a look at what I'm offering at www.kathleenfanningcoaching.com.

Keep well 🙏 ❤️

Kathleen

Day 1

Building
when you need it most!

> "Be comforted, dear soul!
> There is always light behind the clouds."
> ~ Louisa May Alcott

Hope is what we need in abundance in this very strange –and sometimes frightening – time in our history.

I don't really know what the world was like when Louisa May Alcott wrote these words, but they are so apt for today. It can certainly feel as if the world as we knew it has fallen apart but, thankfully, for most of us life continues though in often unpredictable ways.

The message from this is to trust in the future. The world has gone through many changes and has survived – and so will we. The challenge is what kind of world and what part will we play to make it a good one…that's a conversation for another day!

Be well

when you need it most!

Day 1

Draw up a Dream List – a list of what you dream about and what's important to you. Review it and notice is it your list or one you 'inherited' – notice are there many 'shoulds' and does your list really contain your own 'desires' – journal about this.

Building *Resilience*
when you need it most!

Building *Resilience*
when you need it most!

Day 2

Building
when you need it most!

"Oh soul, you worry too much.
You have seen your own strength.
You have seen your own beauty.
You have seen your golden wings.
Why do you worry?"
~ Rumi

Worry is such a senseless thing, yet we spend so much time doing it! I love the word RUMINATION because it sounds like what it is - going over the same thoughts and worries and really getting nowhere.

   Today is a blank slate...we can create what we want. You know deep down you are strong and capable - and how truly gifted you are. Choose to start now to embrace all of you! It will be worth it.

Be well 🙏 ❤️

Day 2

Make a list of your personal strengths or qualities. Look for examples from your life and keep adding to your list! Ask your trusted 'tribe' to contribute.

Building *Resilience* when you need it most!

Day 3

Building Resilience
when you need it most!

> *"It is never too late*
> *to be*
> *what you might have been."*
> ~ George Eliot

Life isn't a dress rehearsal - though it took me a lot of years to realise that. We have just one run at it so why not live the life we want to. It is never too late!

I'm not pretending we have control over many things in our life, what we do have control over is our mind, our thoughts, and our actions.

Listen to your mind chatter and notice how much can be negative. It's not real or true but it can be familiar. When your mind chatter or inner critic has taken hold, breathe, move and even dance! Get out of your head into your body!

Be well

Day 3

Notice your mind chatter today and write about it. Is it more positive or negative? Do you recognize any 'familiar voices' from earlier in your life?
Try moving out of your head when the negative thoughts come in - breathe, move - even dance!

Building *Resilience*
when you need it most!

Building

when you need it most!

Day 4

Building
when you need it most!

"Be open to new ideas,
new experiences
and new adventures
in your life."
~ Anne Devine

Here are two favourites! A beautiful image from Niamh Mason and a beautiful quote from my friend, Anne Devine's book 'Encourage Yourself, Encourage Others'.

How many new ideas, experiences and adventures are you experiencing now? I often use the word Challenge – but isn't Adventure a better term?? For most of us, events in life can challenge our mindset. So many questions without answers! We really do need to have a Growth Mindset which lets us see opportunities and adventures even in these strange times. I don't mean to minimize what's happening and all the uncertainty in the world – but how much easier it will be to move forward if we look at the future with the openness Anne describes. This is what Resilience is really about!

Be well

Day 4

Think back on your life and reflect on the times you have been open to new experiences and adventures. What was that like? Does it contrast to times that you said 'no' to opportunities? What have you learned about your sense of adventure and how might you encourage yourself to say yes more often?!

Building *Resilience*
when you need it most!

Building
Resilience
when you need it most!

Day 5

Building *Resilience*
when you need it most!

> *"Keep your eyes on the stars,
> and your feet on the ground."*
> ~ Theodore Roosevelt

This image is just amazing – it draws our eyes upward to the sky! A metaphor just jumped into my head as I write this – isn't looking skyward a sign of hope?? I think so. It draws our eyes to heaven, to the cosmos and to the changeable weather.

This metaphor prompted a google search and I found a post from a group who had been looking skyward - unsuccessfully - for a recent Super Moon: "It was resilience, in the face of adversity, that kept us all there - soggy and hopeful - that if we hung in there we'd be rewarded. We had planned and teamed up, prepared ourselves, and used the best resources at our disposal, but sometimes that's just not enough to succeed on a given occasion. But it's not a reason not to try again. It's this sort of resilience that is imperative… it is a skill that is developed, not an innate ability.' www.HeathandHoff.com

Finally, Teddy Roosevelt reminds us we need to be dreaming our dreams while being grounded in reality.

Be well 🙏 ❤️

Day 5

Consider if you have a need for predictability and is it serving you or not? Are there opportunities you might embrace if you were to look skyward more? Can you find a balance that enables you to grow?

Building *Resilience*
when you need it most!

Day 6

Building *Resilience*
when you need it most!

> *"Courage is resistance to fear,*
> *mastery of fear,*
> *not absence of fear."*
> ~ Mark Twain

As a child I remember watching a biography of Helen Keller and her amazing life journey – without the advantage of having speech and hearing. It's mind boggling to think how she got over such insurmountable obstacles – but she did and contributed so much over her 88 years. With the help of Anne Sullivan, Helen learned to speak and made a career in both writing and public speaking. Her story is amazing as were her accomplishments. Courageous is an apt description of her - as she worked tirelessly for women's rights, access to education for the visually impaired and those disabled in other ways. She travelled the world sharing her optimism and courage.

She once said, "life is a succession of lessons" and we can't really pick and choose. We are living through them, and we need to trust that we will understand later. Trust is ALL important in times when it feels like we have so little control. But Resiliency is also about making choices and continually pivoting as needed.

A final mention of this beautiful photograph by Niamh Mason – what peace and tranquility it shows. A gift today and every day.

Be well 🙏 ❤️

Day 6

Ask yourself, how are you 'living' the many lessons life is sharing with you? Can you find the gift or opportunity in the challenges that come your way? Is there a mindset shift needed to enable that?

Building *Resilience*
when you need it most!

Day 7

Building *Resilience*
when you need it most!

> *"To have courage for everything*
> *that comes in life –*
> *everything lies in that."*
> ~ Teresa of Avila

Beautiful words and a beautiful image from my favourite photographer!

I'm sure most of us find that some days more courage is needed than others. For me, it's not that that things outwardly change on a given day – but some days it can all just feel more challenging.

Connecting to Resilience, I'm also aware of the importance of good sleep (sometimes a challenge for me), getting exercise and eating well. For me, '2 out of 3 ain't bad' – to quote Meatloaf!! But even when we are doing lots of the right things we can have 'days that demand more courage'. I guess those days call us to be kind and patient with ourselves.

Self-care is another Resilience tool and one many of us neglect. We give freely to others but not always to ourselves. It's not being selfish – we can't give to others what we don't give to ourselves. My Coach challenges us to give ourselves Massive Compassion and it's so needed.

Be well 🙏 ❤️

when you need it most!

Day 7

What is your self-care like? Give yourself a mark out of 10 (0= neglecting yourself and 10 = I'm taking good care of myself!). How might you improve it? Have you noticed a difference in energy when you make time for yourself?

Building *Resilience*
when you need it most!

Building *Resilience*
when you need it most!

Day 8

Building *Resilience*
when you need it most!

> *"Have patience with all things,*
> *but first of all with yourself."*
> ~ Saint Francis de Sales

Another beautiful image from Niamh Mason's collection! Am I a huge fan – yes!!

I found this quote today and it felt like it 'went with' this photograph. Why are we so hard on ourselves – and often criticize ourselves in a way we'd never do to someone else? It is just as well people can't hear when our Inner Critic (or Judge) is on a roll – they'd run a mile! Years ago, I remember someone giving the simple advice that we should speak to ourselves at least as kindly as we'd speak to a stranger – never mind to someone we care about!

Can we 'unlearn' this self-judgement? Yes, and doing so builds up our Resilience muscles. Consistent positive messages are one way to do this as are the type of Mindfulness exercises (PQ reps) we do in Positive Intelligence®. It is possible to shrink the part of the brain where our Judge and Saboteurs 'live' while increasing the size of our Sage or Executive Mind. Exciting stuff!

Our thoughts are something we can control – not easily if we have habitual self-judgement – but with effort we can 'change the tape'. A good friend of mine speaks about a Board of Directors living in our head – and she rightly asks, 'who is the chairperson? Often, it's not our self but someone from childhood! It might be time to retire that chairperson and take the lead our self!

Be well 🙏 ❤️

Building Resilience
when you need it most!

Day 8

Consider who is on your Board of Directors and who might be kindly given a recess or retirement! Reflect on who might be good replacements. They can be people you know and love (past or present) or from film or books – have fun thinking how they might support you!

Building *Resilience* when you need it most!

Building *Resilience*
when you need it most!

Day 9

Building *Resilience*
when you need it most!

> *"Nature does not hurry,
> yet everything is accomplished."*
> ~ Lao Tzu

This rainbow is just one example of the beauty in nature. It reminds me of the hopefulness integral to nature. After the rain – or sometimes during it – the rainbow appears to remind us of what's ahead for us. The seasons are another reminder of the cycle of death and rebirth. The autumn and winter lead to the gift of spring and summer. Nature happens without us rushing it.

What does this tell us about Resilience? With all the many challenges we face, it connects to a few important things: (1) being grounded in the present (not worrying about the future or regretting the past); (2) holding on to a sense of determination to weather a difficult period as best we can and (3) keeping a sense of joy and laughter. That's not all we need but it's worth holding on to each of these. The rainbow will be there after the rain.

Be well 🙏 ❤️

Building
Resilience
when you need it most!

Day 9

Observe your thoughts today and notice are you looking back to the past or to the future. Then at the end of the day, estimate how much of your day was spent in the present moment. Were the past or future thoughts happy or did they create anxiety?

_____
_____
_____
_____
_____
_____
_____
_____
_____
_____
_____
_____
_____

Building *Resilience*
when you need it most!

Building *Resilience*
when you need it most!

Day 10

Building *Resilience*
when you need it most!

> *"It's not what happens to you,*
> *but how you react to it*
> *that matters."*
> ~ Epictetus

This image speaks so strongly of determination and growth – against the odds. I also love these words – challenging though they are. It can feel uncomfortable to think that I/you might be contributing to a negative experience by the way we think or behave but it is true.

   Many of us go through life reacting to events and what other people say or do. Reacting in a 'push button' trigger way rather than choosing our response. Often our emotions lead the way, and we feel hurt, sad, or happy depending on what someone else has done or said. A pattern of 'reacting' to others can create great stress in our system. It's as if we've given the power to someone else to 'decide' what we should think or feel. It takes effort to choose our response and override the trigger reaction. And it calls on us to be aware.

   What I think these words mean is that we need to 'respond' rather than 'react' and the response should be one we are 'happy' with and which is true to our self. Easy peasy – 'fraid not, but worth the effort.

Be well 🙏 ❤️

Building *Resilience* when you need it most!

Day 10

Reflect on the people and situations that 'trigger' you or 'push your buttons'. Begin by just noticing and becoming aware when you react rather than respond. Create a list. Then practice building in a pause to give you time to choose how you want to respond – rather than reacting and perhaps regretting that reaction!

Building *Resilience* when you need it most!

Building *Resilience*
when you need it most!

Day 11

Building *Resilience* when you need it most!

> *"All things must pass.*
> *Strive on diligently.*
> *Don't give up."*
> ~ Buddhist Teaching

Many of us repeat the first line 'All things must pass' as a hopeful mantra – and sometimes out of fear - wanting it to be true. We can experience many highs and lows. It is hard to stay strong, hard to not wonder and really question what is going on and what brought us here?

Our Resilience is always being tested. The rest of this Buddhist saying is so important – 'Strive on diligently. Don't give up.' There will be times when the sadness, anxiety or fear might feel overwhelming. Breathe, take some action like walking, dancing (it works!) or reaching out to someone and I guarantee you'll feel differently in a moment. Our concerns will not have gone away but you will feel a little more able, a little less fearful. The one thing we can count on is change and that nothing stays the same – including or especially our emotions. 'Strive on diligently' and all our baby steps move us forward. 'Don't give up'.

Be well 🙏 ❤

Building Resilience
when you need it most!

Day 11

Consider your Resilience Toolkit – write out a list of your current tools or practices - and reflect on what might be added (breathing, meditation or perhaps gratitude)? Are you ready to commit to a daily routine of these practices? It will pay dividends.

Building *Resilience* when you need it most!

Building
Resilience
when you need it most!

Day 12

Building *Resilience*
when you need it most!

> *"What seems to us as bitter trials are often blessings in disguise."*
> ~ Oscar Wilde

It's hard to think of challenging times as having opportunities but it may be worth 'reframing' this idea. We continually receive helpful tips about creating routines, de-cluttering the house and starting new projects or courses. They are all helpful because they create 'opportunity' when we might be tempted to only focus on the fear and anxiety which is so easy to access.

I'm choosing to be more diligent with my mindfulness practice and know I gain huge benefit from my daily routine. I find the calm and peace I feel in those moments to be helpful. It is helping me to use my breath more consciously – and to appreciate the gift each breath is for me.

We tend to look back and regret missed opportunities. We know thinking this way is pointless, yet our mind often leads us there – but we can direct it to the other 'doors' awaiting us. Optimism pays dividends in mental health and resilience.

Be well 🙏 ❤️

Building *Resilience*
when you need it most!

Day 12

Reflect on your level of optimism on a scale of 0 – 10 (0 I'd describe as Glum Gary and 10 is Optimistic Oliver) – where do you land on the scale? Think of ways you might increase your level of optimism.

Building *Resilience* when you need it most!

Building *Resilience*
when you need it most!

Day 13

Building *Resilience*
when you need it most!

*"We are shaped by our thoughts;
we become what we think.
When the mind is pure, joy follows
like a shadow that never leaves."*
~ Buddha

Niamh Mason's picture has such a calming effect on me. I'm drawn into the tranquility of the water and the beauty of the scene. It makes me think how images can feed us – or disturb us!! Many people do not watch the news for that reason – all the 'bad' news' can have a physical effect on us. I'm not suggesting we block out reality, but we need to protect our minds and hearts. Watch or listen in small doses and, as an antidote, invite more beauty into your life – photographic images, films, books and spending time in nature will help build our resilience. We need to feed our minds and hearts to create the 'bridges to good outcomes'.

Be well 🙏 ❤️

Building Resilience
when you need it most!

Day 13

Mull over what you are 'feeding' yourself – images, media, news – and reflect on how it may be affecting you. Are there boundaries you might set in relation to use of media?

Building *Resilience*
when you need it most!

Building *Resilience*
when you need it most!

Day 14

Building *Resilience*
when you need it most!

*"Start by doing what's necessary,
then do what's possible;
And suddenly you are doing the impossible."*
~ Saint Frances of Assisi

How true is this!!! Just think of all the amazing people we are hearing about daily who are showing us their bravery, their generosity, and their heroism. These people are not just on TV or in the newspaper they are living with us or beside us. History has given us so many examples of how simple kindness impacts lives. I was just reading about a software executive in India who cycles around his city each day to distribute food packets to the poor living on the roadside. He feeds about 50 people each weekday and double that at the weekend.

There are many examples close to our homes. So many good people who give their time - and resources - to make this world better. St. Francis was right – we can even do the impossible!

Be well 🙏 ❤️

Building Resilience
when you need it most!

Day 14

Reflect on the place that kindness has in your life – can it be increased? How might that happen and what would the benefits be?

Building *Resilience*
when you need it most!

Building *Resilience*
when you need it most!

Day 15

Building *Resilience*
when you need it most!

> *"Things do not change;*
> *we change."*
> ~ Henry David Thoreau

I'd say we all spend a good bit of our time focusing on what needs to change – especially in regard to the world we live in. Our thoughts and opinions are certainly valid and often come from wanting things to get better and to get 'better' for people we care about. In his book 'The 7 Habits of Highly Effective People', Steven Covey offers a helpful tool to check where we are putting our focus. He suggests we differentiate between what we are concerned about, what we can influence and then, ultimately, what we can actually control. If you were to make 3 lists, you might find that a lot of your energy goes on what you have little control over or even little influence. What we do have real control over is our thoughts and our actions.

A helpful Resilience tool is to put our time and energy into what we can influence and control. It is draining and stressful to get worked up about what is beyond our control or influence.

The 12 Step Serenity Prayer reflects this beautifully: *'Grant me the Serenity to accept the things I cannot change; the Courage to change the things I can, and the Wisdom to know the difference.'*

Be well 🙏 ❤️

Building *Resilience*
when you need it most!

Day 15

Make the 3 lists mentioned above and be honest to yourself about what goes in each. Give each a % of the real time you give each list. Are there changes you might make from that awareness?

Building *Resilience* when you need it most!

Building
Resilience
when you need it most!

Day 16

Building *Resilience*
when you need it most!

> *"Do not wait;*
> *The time will never be 'just right'.*
> *Start where you stand, and work with*
> *Whatever tools you may have at your command,*
> *And better tools will be found as you go along."*
> ~ George Herbert

A friend recently commented on how technology has contributed to our wellbeing! Zoom, WhatsApp and other Apps help us to stay connected globally to family and friends.

Life brings so many challenging experiences. The ground seems to shift under our feet, and it is continuing to change daily. So, how do you or I 'learn the best way of being myself' in these circumstances??

Resilience in this current time seems to mean pivoting and changing as needed yet feeling that my feet are firmly on the ground. It sounds like a contradiction but it's not. Resilience isn't a magic formula; it's about doing practical things that make you feel grounded and more positive about the future. "It is something you do, rather than something you have."

Be well 🙏 ❤️

Building *Resilience*
when you need it most!

Day 16

Consider the technology in your life and the positive or negative impact each tool may have. Is it time to cut back on-screen time – or remove social media from your phone? What benefit might that bring you?

Building *Resilience*
when you need it most!

Building
Resilience
when you need it most!

Day 17

Building *Resilience*
when you need it most!

*"Every action we take, everything we do,
is either a victory or defeat
in the struggle to become what we want to be."*
~ Ninon de L'Enclos

A favorite exercise of mine is to **consider who is your RoleModel of Resilience.** When I do this in training, I find many people choose to speak about their mothers. My own mother bravely travelled from Ireland to the US with four young children to meet up with my Dad who had left earlier to start a job. She had courage, determination, and optimism - all traits I've since learned contribute to Resilience. She also taught us to be grateful for all we were blessed with - even though she met many challenges along the way.

'*Actions lead to victories or defeats*'. My mother showed me how to be proactive and to be adaptable and flexible.

Be well 🙏 ❤️

Building Resilience
when you need it most!

Day 17

Who is your Role Model of Resilience and what characteristics did s/he have? Bring this person to life on these pages! What can you learn from him or her now?

Building *Resilience* when you need it most!

Building *Resilience*
when you need it most!

Day 18

Building *Resilience*
when you need it most!

> *"Courage is resistance to fear,*
> *mastery of fear,*
> *not absence of fear."*
>
> ~ Mark Twain

Mark Twain's words are certainly relevant today in the world we're living in. I'm so conscious as I write this how blessed I am to be living where I am – in rural Ireland – where I am safe and protected. I'm also grateful that my coaching and training work is primarily online – so I can work with people around the world! I'm also thankful that my husband and I are very healthy. Yet even when things are fine, life always demands courage from us.

    I also know that there are people living near me who must call on their courage each day to do their jobs in the army, police, in hospitals and other settings. I love that the quote says courage is not the absence of fear but the facing of it each and every day. Frontline people always deserve our appreciation and our support.

Be well 🙏 ❤️

Building *Resilience*
when you need it most!

Day 18

Reflect on what the word courage means to you. Think of times in your own life when you were brave and courageous. Anchor those memories in your heart.

Building Resilience
when you need it most!

Building *Resilience*
when you need it most!

Day 19

Building Resilience
when you need it most!

*"Our greatest glory is not in never falling,
but in rising every time we fall."*
~ Confucius

Funny how we can react to different words – and failure is one that I have a strong reaction to. It's just a word and for sure I have not succeeded at everything in my life, but FAILURE seems to have a degree of shame surrounding it?

I love the image and the thought of 'picking myself up and moving forward again' shown in this photograph.

Brené Brown says: "It's not easy or comfortable but grappling with setbacks in life is inevitable. It's natural to stumble and fall when you put yourself out there. There is no shame in making mistakes. And no matter how much it might feel like it is, failure is not the end of the world. The fact that you had the courage to show up and be vulnerable is far more indicative of your character than failure could ever be."

So really it is just a word and what's important is what we do afterwards. Resilience is about picking ourselves up and trying again.

Be well 🙏 ❤️

Building Resilience
when you need it most!

Day 19

Reflect on the experiences in your life that did not go as you would have liked. If you failed, what did you do next and next again? What did you learn through those difficult moments?

Building *Resilience*
when you need it most!

Building
Resilience
when you need it most!

Day 20

Building *Resilience*
when you need it most!

> *"Do not go where the path may lead,*
> *go instead where there is no path*
> *and leave a trail."*
> ~ Ralph Waldo Emerson

We all have heroes who have 'taken the road less travelled'.

This is Resilience. We – I – can play it safe, not take risks and that can be ok…but just ok. What 'achieving greatly' means can vary from one person to another. You need real courage to take the risks – and some people have paid for this with their lives.

Maybe we take risks when we speak our truth and not second guess what others will think of us – or take a step forward and claim a place for our self rather than always waiting to be asked.

Social Media has created a monster of judgment and criticism which young people are particularly vulnerable to. Most of us have an inner critic who judges us harshly enough – without adding the unkind comments that are offered so freely on the internet.

Resilience can help us learn how to manage the inner critic, the Judge– and the self-doubt. A simple start is to not believe everything in our heads – much of it is nonsense we picked up along the way and is not true. Think of how you'd respond to a good friend if you heard them say the same thing – you'd counter it with kindness and reassurance!

Be well 🙏 ❤

Building
Resilience
when you need it most!

Day 20

Is there something you've always wanted to do but it feels too risky? Reflect on what would make it less risky – and how you might make it happen. Remember that courage in your heart!

Building *Resilience* when you need it most!

Building *Resilience*
when you need it most!

Day 21

Building *Resilience*
when you need it most!

*"Have the courage to live each day
to the best of your abilities."*
~ Anne Devine

I have so many favorites from Niamh Mason's images but this one captivates me! It has a real 'Lord of the Rings' quality to it and I am just drawn in. Thank you, Niamh, for allowing me to share your beautiful images.

  I've also taken another quote from Anne Devine's book 'Encourage Yourself, Encourage Others' and I find these words comforting in this time of strangeness, unsettledness and sometimes fear. We are all drawing on courage daily to respond to what the day might bring. I know that my challenges are small compared to others – I say that with gratitude knowing I've been blessed. Be proud of the courage you show.

Be well 🙏 ❤️

Building *Resilience* when you need it most!

Day 21

Do you really know what you are capable of? Reflect on your gifts and abilities and check are you using them as well as you might? How might you stretch yourself today?

Building *Resilience* when you need it most!

Building *Resilience*
when you need it most!

Day 22

Building *Resilience*
when you need it most!

> *"Optimism is the faith
> that leads to achievement.
> Nothing can be done
> without hope and confidence."*
> ~ Helen Keller

This image speaks to me about optimism. Optimism is another Resilience tool and there is a lot of research showing it's good for your health! In 2019 Harvard Medical Journal said that: *"optimism was associated with a 35% lower risk of angina, heart attack, stroke, or death from cardiovascular causes."*

Our brains may be wired for caution and holding on to negative experiences but overall, we are survivors – which could be called Optimism! Put another way, Optimism affects how people react to stressful life events. Specifically, people who are more optimistic are at less risk for anxiety and depression after something stressful happens to them.

Food for thought and something worth cultivating if you happen to be a 'glass half empty' kind of person.

Be well 🙏 ❤️

Building *Resilience*
when you need it most!

Day 22

Think about a person you know well who you'd describe as being optimistic. What does that look like, sound like, feel like for that person? Could you imitate him or her?

Building *Resilience* when you need it most!

Building *Resilience*
when you need it most!

Day 23

Building *Resilience*
when you need it most!

> *"The earth which sustains humanity*
> *must not be injured.*
> *It must not be destroyed."*
> ~ Hildegard of Bingen

We have been operating at such a fast pace, draining the earth's resources and not paying heed to the climatic changes that we are experiencing already. Our world is exhausted – as are many of us – and it would be a terrible shame if changes in lifestyle, consumption and respect for this planet did not follow from all this awareness.

From the 11th century Hildegard calls to us to protect and nurture 'the earth which sustains humanity'. There are important choices we need to make, and we need to build up our resilience to get through this time – and move forward sustainably.

Be well 🙏 ❤️

Building *Resilience* when you need it most!

Day 23

Take stock of how you are 'minding' or caring for this world of ours. Are you cutting down on plastic, fossil fuels and waste? Is there more you might do? The <u>Sustainable Development Goals</u> spell out how we can protect our environment and slow climate change, from forests to oceans to everywhere in between. Think about your electricity use and your travel. Check your dinner table. Reuse whatever you can. The possibilities for action are many – and each make a difference.

Building *Resilience* when you need it most!

Building *Resilience*
when you need it most!

Day 24

Building *Resilience*
when you need it most!

> *"Happiness is when what you think,*
> *what you say and*
> *what you do are in harmony."*
> ~ Mahatma Gandhi

These words – and Niamh Mason's image speak to me today. It is so challenging to live congruently – to have our actions reflect our values. Sometimes we need the support of others to do this.

  Courage can mean knowing when we need to reach out for support. Many of us find it hard to ask for help or support yet willingly give it to others. Perhaps it's time to let others 'gift' us with their support now too.

Be well 🙏 ❤️

Building Resilience
when you need it most!

Day 24

How accepting are you of help or support from others? Are you good at giving it and not so good at taking it? Think this through on your Journal pages and consider opportunities for letting others give to you.

Building *Resilience* when you need it most!

Building
Resilience
when you need it most!

DAY 25

Building *Resilience*
when you need it most!

> *"When it comes to life the critical thing is whether you take things for granted or take them with gratitude."*
> ~ GK Chesterton

I'd love to say to myself - and to you - that you've suffered enough and there are only good times ahead, but you'd easily see the flaw in that. There are no guarantees in life and we are continually shown how little control we have.

As mentioned earlier, Stephen Covey suggests we focus on what we can control and/or influence and not waste our energy on what's out of our control. There is real wisdom in that approach. Life doesn't get easier, but our mindset can change and we can become more Resilient by building a practice that fills that well on a daily basis. Good sleep, hydration, exercise, positive thinking, gratitude and meditation are the key practices that make us stronger and more resilient. It's all in our hands!

Be well 🙏 ❤️

Building Resilience
when you need it most!

Day 25

Reflect on your attitude to life. Are you disappointed with aspects of it? What energy are you still using on situations that are not in your control or even influence? Refocus on what is in your control!

Building *Resilience*
when you need it most!

Building
Resilience
when you need it most!

Day 26

Building *Resilience*
when you need it most!

> *"Great works are performed
> not by strength but by perseverance."*
> ~ Samuel Johnson

This is my photo of a favourite tree taken on our regular walk along the River Suir in Cahir, Tipperary. This tree is battered by wind, rain and sometimes flooded by the river yet it survives. In life, being rigid like an oak might sound strong and able but without flexibility – and perseverance we are in danger of being knocked down by events.

'Go with the flow' is a cliche but also a truth. There are times to be strong and upright in our truth and beliefs and we may weather the storm by doing that. On the other hand, many times in life being flexible and adaptable enables us to do more than survive. Resilience means learning from the difficult experience and, sometimes, it means owning our own part in what happened. Strength to the point of rigidness may give us a sense of being 'right' but that can often be a poor consolation.

Be well 🙏 ❤️

Building *Resilience*
when you need it most!

Day 26

When a trigger of negative emotion comes, focus on your breath, or get up and move around. Notice how you can shift into a more neutral or even positive space. Look for moments of joy. Is there room for more laughter? We tend to be so, so serious! Think of ways you can bring more lightness in.

Building *Resilience*
when you need it most!

Building
Resilience
when you need it most!

Day 27

Building *Resilience*
when you need it most!

*"When you do things from your soul,
you feel a river moving in you, a joy."*
~ Rumi

I have always found Rumi's words to be amazingly apt and true. Whatever our spiritual beliefs, our 'soul' seems to be our authentic, wise self. When we act from that best place it is so different from acting from the fear and worry that the survival part of our brain portrays as reality.

We have a choice - embrace the power that is in each of us or continue to live in a fearful place. That sounds harsh as I write it, but I am at a point in my life when I've finally realised what's important and what is in my control.

Be well 🙏 ❤️

Building Resilience
when you need it most!

Day 27

Today consider how you are 'grounding yourself' in the midst of the storm that life can be. Are you in the present and are you finding joy in the moment?

Building *Resilience*
when you need it most!

Building *Resilience*
when you need it most!

Day 28

Building *Resilience*
when you need it most!

*"Resilience is the ability
to find the inner strength to bounce back
from a set-back or challenge."*
~ Unknown

How amazing we are and how often we do bounce back from setbacks and challenges! Despite those successes, we tend to focus on our mistakes or feel let down when we seem to not be coping well. In his book Positive Intelligence®, Shirzad Chamine speaks of our mind being 'our best friend. It can also be our worst enemy'. It takes effort to manage the survival part of our brain that misguidedly thinks it protects us by pointing out the worst possible outcomes.

Getting into our senses, focusing on our breath, movement and gratitude are a few ways to develop the Sage or wise part of our brain. That is where we find the inner strength to bounce back and so much more!

Be well 🙏 ❤️

Building
Resilience
when you need it most!

Day 28

Reflect on the people and situations that 'trigger' you or 'push your buttons'. Begin by just noticing and becoming aware of times that you react rather than respond. Create a list and commit to defusing the triggers by awareness.

Building *Resilience*
when you need it most!

Building
Resilience
when you need it most!

Day 29

11

Building *Resilience*
when you need it most!

> *"If you hit a wall,*
> *climb over it,*
> *crawl under it,*
> *or dance on top of it."*
> ~ Unknown

I have rediscovered dance and the benefits it can bring to my life. While I may harbor a dream of ballroom dancing with my husband (!), now I'm happy to be dancing on my own to Beyonce, Jason Timberlake and some of my golden oldie favourites!

Dance improves mood, lowers stress and anxiety - and it's fun. Dance is a lovely metaphor for life too. It can be enjoyable to observe beautiful dancers - or aspects of life- but there is little real growth happening when we stay sitting watching on the side-lines of life. Change is an ever-present part of life, and we can watch it from a distance or 'plunge in, move with it and join the dance'!

Be well 🙏 ❤️

Building *Resilience*
when you need it most!

Day 29

Re-read your 'trigger' list and consider how you might like to change your response. Consider one that brings a habitual negative reaction and be prepared to count to 10, take a deep breath or use some strategy that creates a pause - allowing you to choose how you want to respond.

Building *Resilience*
when you need it most!

Building *Resilience*
when you need it most!

Day 30

Building *Resilience*
when you need it most!

"Courage is in 'encouragement' for a reason.
Encourage others to be brave.
Tell them, 'You can make it.'
Tell this to yourself too."

~ Anne Devine
Author: Encourage Yourself & Encourage Others

Thank you for accompanying me in this reflective 30 Days of Resilience Journal. I am sure you had days that the reflection happened easily and others where you worked hard on staying with the process.

   Please acknowledge your successes and encourage yourself to go forward. Building our Resilience is not really a 30 Day 'job'. It may involve changing some of our less helpful habits and creating new healthy ones. Taking stock of what we are doing well and what could be improved is a cause of celebration. We need to acknowledge each and every time we 'invest in ourselves' and in our wellbeing and resilience. We are showing bravery.

   Encouraging ourselves and others to be brave and to keep trying is what we are called to do - it's good for all of us!

Be well 🙏 ❤️

Building *Resilience*
when you need it most!

Day 30

Today - observe, are you reacting or responding? What situation might you focus on to change your response – and practice! Notice your successes with this too!

Building *Resilience*
when you need it most!

Building *Resilience*
when you need it most!

FINAL WORDS

I'm delighted that you have made this 30 Day journey with me and I hope that you are feeling the benefit of the new tools and the reflections. It takes up to 90 days to really create new habits but by following these 30 days you have started to embed some new practices and a new level of awareness.

I wish you all the best and I hope that you continue to keep your Well of Resilience Filled!

Kathleen 🙏 ❤️

Building
Resilience
when you need it most!

ABOUT KATHLEEN FANNING

Kathleen is a Professional Certified Coach with the International Coach Federation and has been awarded the Coach of the Year, 2023 by ICF Ireland. She has many years' experience as a coach and trainer specializing in supporting women in leadership who are experiencing overwhelm, near burn out and that sense of 'never accomplishing all they want to do'. Find out more about Kathleen and what she offers on www.kathleenfanningcoaching.com

She'd be delighted to share a 'virtual cuppa' with you. Reach out to kathleen@kathleenfanningcoaching.com to arrange a chat.

https://www.linkedin.com/in/kathleen-fanning/
https://www.facebook.com/KFanningCoaching
Twitter: @KFanningCoach
https://www.instagram.com/fanning.kathleen/

Printed in Great Britain
by Amazon